"A MOTHER'S JOURNEY"

A Story of Drugs, Suicide and Survival

"A MOTHER'S JOURNEY"

A Story of Drugs, Suicide and Survival

Deborah Doppelt

ISBN: 978-1-956074-36-9 (Paperback Edition)
ISBN: 978-1-956074-37-6 (Hardcover Edition)
ISBN: 978-1-956074-35-2 (E-book Edition)

Book Ordering Information

Phone Number: 315 288-7939 ext. 1000 or 347-901-4920
Email: info@globalsummithouse.com
Global Summit House
www.globalsummithouse.com

Printed in the United States of America

INTRODUCTION

I was an elementary physical education and health teacher in a private Parochial school in New Jersey. I believe in a healthy mind and body. Josh passed away at the age of twenty three and this story is based on actual journal entries made shortly after his death and continuing until today.

This book is a celebration of my son Josh's life; the treasured times as well as the heartbreaking ones. My story is that of a young man whose life was cut short just before reaching the prime of his life. A life filled with love, hope, anger and forgiveness. The following sections are filled with information regarding his childhood, teen years and young adulthood. I trust you as readers will learn from our heartfelt yet flawed actions. If this will help one family out there it will have been worth it. This is intended as a guide for all junior and senior high school students and their parents. I believe some teenagers do not have the ability to understand the consequences of their actions. Suicide; accidental or not leaves a devastating and permanent scar on the loved ones they leave behind.

In Jill Bialosky's book "HISTORY OF A SUICIDE," she quotes psychiatrist Andrew Slaby as stating *"Suicide attempts are really failed suicides."* She also states that *"according to statistics, about a third of people who attempt suicide will repeat the attempt within one year and about 10 percent of those who threaten or attempt suicide eventually succeed in carrying out the act. It is remarkable how many failed suicide precede an actual suicide."*

Phil Donahue has stated that *"Suicide is a permanent solution to a temporary problem."*(Internet)

THE FIVE STAGES OF GRIEF

1. Denial
2. Anger
3. Bargaining
4. Depression
5. Acceptance

In our bereavement, we spend different lengths of time working through each step and express each stage more or less intensely. The five stages do not necessarily occur in order. We often move between stages before achieving a more peaceful acceptance of death. Many of us are not afforded the luxury of time required to achieve this final stage of grief. Throughout each stage, a common thread of hope emerges. As long as there if life, there is hope. As long as there is hope, there is life." Julie Axelrod (Internet)

CHAPTER ONE

DENIAL

"The first reaction to learning of a death is to deny the reality of the situation. It is a normal reaction to rationalize overwhelming emotions. It is a defense mechanism that buffers the immediate shock. We block out the words and hide from the facts. This is a temporary response that carries us through the first wave of pain." Julie Axelrod. First proposed by Elsabeth Kubler-Ross in her 1969 book

"On Death and Dying"

The Phone Call

January 4th 2008

6:30-7:00 am

Upon arriving at school this morning I followed my usual routine as I am one of the first teachers in the building. I turned on the lights in my office and the gym then my computer. I was very nervous after speaking to Josh on New Year's Eve as he seemed somewhat preoccupied. I was not sure what he was truly feeling. He was not always honest in his emotions so how could I be sure as he was living in Florida? I checked my e-mail I saw his name on the list of entries and immediately opened his letter. He began in an upbeat manner, stating he promised to turn his misguided life around. As his letter continued it became darker and more depressing. I believe he finally realized the errors of his ways and thought there was absolutely no way out of this quagmire he had developed for himself. Hopelessness encompassed him.

10:00 am

He never confided in us that he was thinking about suicide. I now believe it was an accident as he always had a flair for the dramatic. I do suppose it was a cry for help as his attempt of taking Oxycodone, Xanax and Methadone had been tried a few weeks earlier but without any detrimental effects. (We did not know this fact until much later included in a letter he left behind.) He did leave a few angry letters to girlfriends and family members. I chose not to read any of them as I believe he was not thinking clearly and I wished to remember him in a somewhat positive manner.

I never use my cell phone during class time as I believe it inappropriate, however, this morning was different. I knew something was wrong –call it mother's intuition. My dog walker called and said *"the police are at your house looking for Jerry."* Why were they looking for my husband? It had to be important news. The time from my home to school is about fifteen minutes -I paced constantly. The waiting period was excruciating as many scenarios played out in my head. I did not know if my son was alive or perhaps hurt in some kind of accident. I prayed for the latter.

I knew whatever they wanted was not good. I immediately dismissed my preschool class and made several calls to the police station. They would not release any information over the phone. Their response was repeated again and again *"Captain Deuer and another officer are on their way"*.

A duo of police cars pulled into our parking lot and panic took over my body. I wanted to hear what was wrong but yet I did not want to know! The cars pulled in front of the gym with my husband and time stood still as a "snapshot in my minds eye". I remember where I was, what I was wearing and what I was doing, as in the case of the JFK was assassination.

Our school was supposed to have a first Friday liturgy at 10:30 which was canceled on my behalf. I could not understand at the time why classes were not coming into our building. Our campus is comprised of three buildings. One housing the primary department grades k-3 and specials (art and physical education), one intermediate grades 4-5 and pre-school and the junior high grades 6, 7, 8. The tradition is that each upper grade assists in walking a lower grade to the church and back after mass.

Jerry walked into my office crying and I begged *"please tell me he is ok, please tell me he's ok. Please tell me he's in the hospital and not dead."* Jerry shook his head and said *"he's gone!"* I was sobbing and shaking uncontrollably. How could this be happening to us, we were good parents? I lost track of time. I believe hours passed as it took me that long to gather myself. At this point our priest, the principal and office staff were trying their best to console me. As luck would have it the priest from our school is friendly with our rabbi and had his cell number in his phone. We left our school and were driven home by the police to begin the funeral arrangements.

CHAPTER TWO
MY EARLY YEARS

I am a product of two devoted, loving parents who were always dedicated to us and each other. My mother was a housewife and my father was a businessman. All they ever wanted was for my brother and I to have the best life possible. This was accomplished by a tough work ethic and always having family time to discuss our days. My brother and I got into a lot of mischief back then when children were allowed to go out and play with other neighborhood children. We came home when we were hungry, the street lights came on or when our mother would open the door and yell for us. We had squabbles with other children but we learned how to work things out. Today most children have structured play dates and activities; they do not know how to give and take. They are on the computer, cell phone or playing video games with little or no interaction with other children.

Of course, my brother and I had some sibling rivalry as children but we have now grown up with mutual respect for one another. One of my fondest memories was playing "king of the mountain" with our dad. The goal of this activity was to pull him off their king size bed- we went through many mattresses in those days!!

I truly grew up in "the wonder years" in the mid-late 60's, graduating high school in 1969. There were troubles in the world -Viet Nam, drugs and the sexual revolution, however, I was not touched personally by these events. My school years were spent in a fairly large town and high school; summers were spent at the Jersey shore where we had a family home. These were the best times of my life; days were spent on the beach, we played football on our front lawn until nightfall (often using car headlights to keep the game going!) We had beach parties for our town friends (the riskiest thing we did was to put beer in soda cans). Most evenings were spent just enjoying each other's company taking turns at our various houses.

My closest friends to this day are from this small shore town. We all grew up and went in different directions – getting married, getting divorced, having children, losing parents as well as children (in my case.) However, we still manage to stay in touch-it may not be every week or month but we always knew that if we needed each other we would be there! Looking back in time I don't think we appreciated what a great era it truly was.

Getting Married

I am the first born in my family, followed two years later by my brother Alan. We came from a non-practicing Catholic family. We celebrate Christmas and Easter only as a means to have a large holiday dinner with friends and family. These days are not religiously observed.

Upon marrying my husband I converted to Judaism as his religion is the stronger of the two. I even kept a kosher home and observed all holiday traditions. I was eager to learn about Judaism and its relevance to Christianity. I have learned many interesting historical as well as religious lessons along the way as I studied once a week for a year one on one with a rabbi from Clifton, N.J. This instruction was interesting as we covered the year by its holidays and their importance. I completed my schooling, complete with a "Mikvah" a Jewish, cleansing bath.

Jews and Italians are very similar in their traditions; mothers are always pushing food and guilt! Family is always in the forefront, equally important to each side. Our families were very compatible, even traveling on vacation together. Both families were involved in retail sales and understood each other well. It was a very unique situation.

JOURNAL ENTRY

4/3/08

Dear Josh,

I don't know where to begin as this is my first time journaling. One of the parents from my school gave me this journal. I am not sure what I am supposed to write as I never had a diary growing up. I was more of the tomboy type, climbing trees and playing outside was more to my liking. I have been told that writing thoughts down on paper will be helpful- I'm not too sure about this but I will give it a try. You had the world at your fingertips. What went so horribly wrong? I had a horrible day yesterday, today seems to be starting better. I cried all morning as the depression sets in a few times a week and just doesn't want to pass. I don't want to shop, cook or clean as your death really hit us hard. Jordan is beginning therapy tomorrow and I have gone twice so far.

I went to my therapist today. When I talk about you and all the foolish things you have done she must think you were so confused and lost. But you are our son; you have a face, a name and a personality, however wrong or twisted that personality may be.

I cannot function during the day at all; I go through the motions and take my classes like a robot. I hide in my office and cry during any free time that I may have. Upon coming home I try to follow a routine but nothing gets accomplished. I don't know what's right anymore, actually I do know; dad and I always said "*he'll snap out of it one day*", but those days came and went as you got older and things only became worse. The lies, the playing me against your father; you only were able to mature to a certain point and were never able to move on. I think I am finally able to get angry at you as I think back to all the chances you had and just could not make the correct one.

- MOM

JOURNAL ENTRY

4/7/08

Dear Josh,

I was looking through the Mother's day cards you sent over the years and I have saved every one of them. On that day in 2007 you wrote (from a rehab facility in Fla.) in an already beautifully worded card... you stated *"Although it is hard for me to express my feelings, I hope you know how much I truly do appreciate all your love and support through these difficult times. I love you with all my heart and wish you the best Mother's day."*

- *Love Josh*

4/9/08

Dear Josh,

I'm feeling a bit better today, taking two classes over to the oval to run. Dad got a call from the Palm Beach sheriff's office today-Robert R. was caught yesterday and will be charged with dealing drugs. Dad was very instrumental in playing detective, as he constantly was in touch with the police in Florida and would not give up until Robert R. was in custody. Too bad you didn't have the strength or determination to stay away from him. You had a good life; you came from normal, quality families. I guess you just couldn't see the forest for the trees.

4/10/08

Dear Josh,

I wonder how much more meaning your life could have had if you had taken the straight path. It took much more effort to get involved in all of this mess. But in your mind you just couldn't get it. We made plans for your unveiling for June 29th. (We never did have one; after about one year we visited the cemetery on our own).

4/14/08

Josh,

We went up to Ithaca this past weekend to see Jordan. The three and a half hour ride was torturous; I cried all the way up there, however, I was better on the way home. Just being in the car with your mind wandering is so difficult.

The principal of my school wants to plant a tree on the property in your honor along with a prayer service. I went to my therapist today and she stated that perhaps you decided to leave us because you didn't want to hurt us anymore or possibly that you did not want to be in mental anguish any longer.

4/22/08

Dear Josh,

I saw my therapist yesterday and after the meeting I felt somewhat better. I also had a dream about you last night.

- Love, mom

4/25/08

So depressed, so depressed, so depressed!!!

5/12/08

Dear Josh,

Had a horrible mother's day yesterday…so emotionally angry and mixed up. At least now you are at peace but we are a mess!!!

5/22/08

Dear Josh,

Today is poppy's 80th birthday. Jordan is in Israel visiting your memorial that Uncle Steve and Aunt Carol had made. It is a beautiful plaque positioned on a stone in the Botanical Garden in Haifa. She said it was great to see and today of all days we had a prayer service and a tree planting outside my office. The weather in the morning was threatened by rain. However, as the service approached the sky cleared and the sun came out in all its glory. You never did like bad weather.

Your "dogwood tree "is quite unique as it is a hybrid. Its colors are a bright pink on one side and white on the other. The prayer is worded: "Be present with us today to remember Joshua and his life through the planting of this tree. May this tree speak the power of your life? In the midst, deeply rooted and ever growing in all creation Amen."

Dad and Aunt Jude came – Dad and I cried as did many teachers and students. Why did you do this to us?? I had my first panic attack today; it was extremely frightening as I did not know what was happening to me. Was it a stroke or heart attack? I began to shake, stutter and had a hard time catching my breath. The more I tried to breath the harder it became. One teacher from our school happened to walk by my office and saw what was happening to me. An ambulance was called and I was taken to the hospital for tests on EEG's, EKG's which showed nothing but a panic attack from the stress of the day. I was released a few hours later.

- Love Mom

CHAPTER THREE

JOSH'S EARLY YEARS

Josh was born March 27th 1984 in Livingston, N.J. He was our first child, born full term at 9lbs 1 ounce and was given a proper Apgar- birth score (a rating for newborns). The next day he began turning blue and was diagnosed with a seizure disorder easily remedied by Phenobarbital but came home on a fetal heart monitor in case of SIDS (Sudden Infant Death Syndrome). A strap with wires attached to it had to be connected to his chest every evening before bed. Whenever he moved during his sleep the alarm would go off. We would run to his room not knowing what to expect. These episodes were all false alarms stemming from the wires not being connected properly. We were worried parents did not sleep much at that time. The medicine was stopped at about the age of nine months.

I vividly recall one afternoon when Josh and I fell asleep

on our den couch which was covered in an ugly orange and brown floral print but it was extremely comfortable. Josh was never a good sleeper in the evenings, waking up quite often. This particular afternoon, he was nuzzled under my chin and on my chest. I lied down with him while the afternoon sun shown through the windows filling our den with sunshine and warmth. We fell asleep together for more than an hour. I can still smell the fresh baby powder that emanated from his warm, small body. He always held a cloth diaper to his face for comfort; we called it his "schmuggle" just like the character in *Peanuts.*

He grew normally; hitting all the milestones young children do, however, Josh was always inquisitive and a bit too daring. Always pushing our limits-if we said no he would wear us down until he got what he wanted. Our family always said; Josh would be a great prosecuting attorney because he always won the arguments!!

Josh was stubborn to a fault, angry for no reason at times and generally quite a handful. At about the age of six (he confessed to me much later in life) he began liking the taste of grape Tylenol and would have them on occasion even when he was not ill. As I now recall certain facts, I realize all the little signs I missed along the way. When he was younger, while looking for an item in our linen closet I would find things out of place and just thought these items were not returned properly. In actuality it was Josh seeking the grape Tylenol. This was probably a first clue as to his predisposition to liking drugs.

Josh had many temper tantrums as a child, sometimes as many as three or four in a day. The least little thing would set him off. I remember these occurrences happening when he was about two years old as he was quite a handful in those days. There were times that he did not want to go to school or to a local day camp in the summer. He always needed to be coaxed to go but afterward he would come home saying he had a great time.

CHAPTER FOUR

The Surgeries

8/5/08

Josh,

This has been a tough summer as I had right shoulder surgery on a Thursday, June 25th resulting in my inability to write or type. Two days later on Saturday; your sister's twenty-first birthday, I complained only of confused thoughts and actions and believed it was a result of the pain medicine. I did not experience any headaches or dizziness of any kind. I wanted to write a certain word but it came out totally different. On a few occasions thoughts would just leave my head, I attributed this sensation to your death. I did not want to do anything that would interfere with Jordan's party so we told her that we were just going to the hospital because I was not feeling well.

I was taken to St. Barnabas Hospital in Livingston NJ where an MRI was performed. The doctors discovered a large (grapefruit sized) brain tumor. I was sent home for a few days on steroids hoping to shrink the mass. I entered the hospital four days later on July 3rd (six months to the day of your death) and underwent a nine hour surgery. The operation was successful as it was a benign Menigioma (a jelly-like) growth that had formed on the outside of my brain. It was situated in the front, left side of my skull. The scar from the incision is similar to the stitching on a baseball! I was not able to speak correctly for approximately three weeks, my thoughts were correct but were verbalized in a mixed order or not at all coherent. This may have been a reaction to the medications or swelling around my brain from the surgery. Jordan was the only person who understood me and could translate my "disjointed language."

- Love, Mom

I was placed in the ICU for twenty-four hours and monitored constantly. I felt as if I was in solitary confinement, as the room was cold and sterile. Only one or two visitors were allowed at a time as the doctors did not want me to become excited or agitated. The nurses checked on my comfort level regularly along with giving me prescribed medicine (even during the little sleep I could get!)My days were filled with intermittent cat naps. I remember waking from one of these naps thinking it must be the next day, however, only a few hours had passed. My nights consisted of alarms ringing and monitors beeping. Sleeping was a problem as I was uncomfortable and aggravated with my condition. I was not even allowed to get off the bed to go to the bathroom! In my drugged stupor, I heard a very annoying bubbling sound that made it difficult to sleep. An exasperating amount of time passed where I tried in vain to explain what I was hearing. Remember; I was not able to speak coherently for another three weeks. My sister-in-law finally realized it was the oxygen gurgling next to my bed.

I recall another morning, after being transferred to a regular room, being very frustrated after the surgery. My right arm was useless, my head was hurting and I was dazed and confused. I called for the nurse to assist me in straightening my sling, however, she was unable to as it was complicated in its design. I called for my sister-in-law who is also a nurse and she immediately came to my rescue. My conversation went like this, *"Jude, help-stuck!"* She rushed right over not knowing what to expect! I tried to explain my situation as best as I could, however, just seeing me explained it all. I felt like*" a one armed paper hanger!"* She was my savior as she immediately untwisted the sling and made me comfortable again as I couldn't even straighten myself properly on the bed. This situation was extremely aggravating for me as I am a very independent woman and not used to having to ask for help. I could not even feed myself without assistance.

I was released from the hospital at the end of the week and now had to begin painful physical therapy for my shoulder. This would last at least eight weeks. I was driven back and forth to therapy by an aide who was my lifesaver as she also helped with the cooking and cleaning. This was extremely frustrating for me as I even needed help showering.

I was forced to keep my hair short for next 6-8 months and was destined to wear baseball caps even when I was finally able to return to work.

Before the surgery I had medium length straight blonde hair then afterward; the top was shaved and the back was long. The sight of me in the mirror was disturbing and depressing. My hairdo was then a combination of a mullet and "Gallagher" the comedian whose trademark is smashing watermelons with a sledge hammer.

Even though the brain surgery was a success; the doctors had to operate two more times as the first incision became infected. This was followed by my having to take six weeks off from school to be on a PIC line (intro-venous anti-biotic). I remember walking into the temple for Rosh

Hashanah after the second surgery wearing a beret so no one could see the hideous indentation in my head. I would wake up in the morning and my head would appear normal, however as the day progressed my scalp would collapse like a deflated football. That holiday everyone in Shull looked at me wondering if I was a cancer patient going through chemotherapy or radiation. I wanted to *"parachute off of a dime"*. At the end of six weeks I had the final third surgery to replace that small part of my scull with a plastic plate. I was now able to return to work. It has been six months of hell.

CHAPTER FIVE

Anger

Josh enjoyed his early years of pre-school and elementary school where he participated in sports along with class plays where he was quite the ham. His out-going, strong willed nature surfaced in regard to having to be in charge. His hazel/blue eyes, dimples and blonde hair (as a child) allowed him to charm most children as well as adults. I happily awaited his entrance into our home describing his days at school.

His early summers were spent at local day camps and the shore on weekends. As Josh grew older he attended a sports camp about an hour away. He also had the opportunity one summer to travel to Europe on a teen tour. We received pictures from him from various places. In one such picture he was unrecognizable as his usually brown hair was bleached blonde! I recall receiving a phone call from him: "*Mom- I broke a mirror in the hotel room.*" "*How did it happen?*" I asked. He said "*I was fooling around with one of the other kids and it broke.*" I am sure there was more to this story.

Josh was an average student in elementary school with a few phone calls from the teachers stating he could try harder and needed to stay focused. He didn't have many friends as they would come and go; never a best friend that most children have today. He was always a dramatist by that I mean if he fell he would act as if he were dying, exaggerating the situation. In a 5th grade P.E. class he injured his leg outside on the playground, the nurse brought out an office type wheel chair, I was notified and the end result was that he was fine.

Perhaps this over dramatization of injuries stemmed from our other child (a younger daughter) being very ill with a seizure disorder beginning and 18 months and lasting until she was about 5 yrs old. Whenever she developed a fever from an ear infection or strept throat she would have a seizure most times lasting a few minutes. My husband would always park our car facing the street because we knew a trip to the emergency room was imminent. These were very frightening to us as parents and especially to Josh as he did not understand the nature of the event- he only knew she would end up in the emergency room and stay in the hospital for a few days. During a bout with chicken pox she needed to be transferred to St.

Joseph's Hospital in Paterson. On this occasion she was given too much valium and stopped breathing and had to be intebated; a breathing tube had to be inserted down her throat. Josh usually stayed with relatives while my husband and I took turns at the hospital. These were definitely traumatic times for a young boy.

JOURNAL ENTRY

10/9/09

Dear Josh

It has been over a year since I have written, I am not sure why! Maybe life got in the way. I have had several panic attacks this past year. My doctors call it a tic (not a seizure). Sometimes I am able to push your dying into my subconscious for a while but then it usually surfaces with one of the attacks.

I still cannot grasp that you are no longer with us. I am not a religious woman, nor did I come from a religious home. However, the older I become the more spiritual I have become. Perhaps this is due to your death.

I find comfort in believing in events such as; dimming lights, door bells that ring with no one there, the buzzer in my gym rang with no electricity attached to it and your cell phone rang two times while turned off. Lights in our kitchen have dimmed as well as a light in your sister's car (no the bulbs were not about to go out).

A few years ago dad and I were recommended to a *"medium"* in NY City. We did not offer too much information, just that you had passed away and your age. She told us facts that were astounding and to which no-one could possibly know. At one point she began to move and act like you. We came away dazed, crying and utterly amazed. She knew your personality, character and faults and kept repeating *"I didn't mean for this to happen"-I am so sorry! "I didn't mean for this to happen"-I am so sorry".* Another point during our conversation she said *"I see two eggs."* We were stunned as we recalled a Passover with Grandpa Irving before he passed away in 1996. Since then we have had a special tradition where a dish of hard boiled eggs is placed on the Seder table (among other items). Grandpa never wanted his egg cracked by accident; only he could accomplish this. Since his death and in his honor we always have an "un-cracked egg" in the center of the holiday table. When the *"medium"* said I see two eggs we interpreted this to mean you want your egg with your grandfather's.

Josh, I met a woman recently who wrote a book about her daughter who had passed away from leukemia eleven years ago. We had many stories in common and could have talked for hours, upon leaving she suggested that I "channel" you in my thoughts and go home and begin seriously writing your story. I was encouraged to do this as she recommended so I set up my computer in our den and poured myself a glass of wine. Jordan called and said *"I have left our house too early to go to my friend's party."* So she was returning home for a little while. Within twenty minutes after her return the front door opened, we asked *"Who is there*? "No answer, no footsteps. We asked again and still the same empty response. The police were called to check the house, nothing was amiss. Josh I know you were there; as Josh Groban sings so beautifully *"I feel you all around me, your energy so clear."*

Some of these events can be explained logically however, in my heart I need to believe you are reaching out to us. I guess we will never know what is waiting for us *"on the other side."*

My principal had a good idea at a faculty meeting today, she expressed that when something is suppressed in one's mind if you write about it –it brings those feelings to the surface.

I miss you so much- we have a great picture of you in the den. It's so "you" I am looking at it now while I'm writing this and crying. People at school think I am so strong. My kids are my little therapists as they help me get through each day. The people I work with have been wonderful to me. Miss you so much.

- Love –Mom

JOURNAL ENTRY

10/10/09

Dear Josh

Dad and I often disagree on whether we should talk about you or not. It makes me feel better but not him. He's afraid I'll be hurt by any conversation about you; however, I said *"it would eventually help me."* We never really know how to handle things. It's so easy to say he's in a safe place now and out of pain. But that's nonsense you had choices and you made the worst possible choice!!! We all will never be the same.

10/11/09

Dear Josh

I went to a friend's daughter's bridal shower today at

a local country club. The room was beautifully decorated with colorful flower arrangements. I managed to survive the cocktail hour as it was cheerful with lots of small talk.

My presence there was expected as I am very friendly with the family. I sat with a few women that I knew and they seemed friendly enough. I was very uncomfortable being in this setting as I knew the small talk would eventually center on children. The conversations began with different women trying to outdo each other as to the various stages of their children's "perfect" lives. I anxiously and nervously awaited my turn. I wished to be anywhere but in that room at that time. Finally, when asked "*how many children do you have*?" I answered "*two but one passed away.*" That was the end of the conversation! I was extremely uncomfortable at this point. I stayed a little while but made my departure prematurely and cried all the way home arriving in time to watch the 2nd half of the Giants game. I needed that distraction. I **MISS** our texting during the games!! I miss you so much but writing helps me feel somewhat connected to you.

Jordan graduated from Ithaca and is working as a paralegal in a law firm in Roseland. She is still thinking about going to law school; however, is content and very happy working at the law office.

I really find that writing to you helps so much-I sit in the den and look at your picture (its sooooo you).

- Love Mom

10/12/09

Dear Josh,

I was off from school today, for Christopher Columbus.

The day was spent quietly, and I will return to work tomorrow. I cannot believe you will be gone two years; dad and I aren't sure what to do about Thanksgiving this year. Last year was the last time you were here with us and we don't know if we can handle it. I look at the pictures from last Thanksgiving as I keep them in my purse and I always wear the necklace Grandma Josie gave you of the "schma" (Hebrew) prayer. I called your roommate from Florida to see if he could locate this necklace. I was frantic as I desperately wanted this keepsake. We couldn't find it for a while but St. Anthony came through for me and I found it in your room. I must have walked past it several times- I believe you must have brought it home at some point. I never take it off!!! Love you,

- Mom

10/18/09

Dear Josh,

Dad and I went to Nero's last night. The waiters sang happy birthday to a girl a few tables away from us. I thought immediately of how we took you there for your birthdays since you were five and how you always wore a jacket and tie. It was a dinner of very mixed emotions as seated next to us was a young boy named Josh –I cried all the way home.

10/29/09

Dear Josh,

I have been very sad as of late. Last evening Jordan and dad did "legs up-legs down". This reminded me of you so much as we did this all the time when you were young. Of course I made them stop and I began to cry.

Little things happen during the course of my days that strike a chord in me. A song on the radio; a conversation on the phone; a movement or gesture by one of my students; a picture of a beach on TV are constant reminders of you. You always loved the shore. I remember you "boogie-boarding" in the ocean trying to catch the waves as they crashed toward the water's edge. Do you remember sitting on poppy's lap driving the tractor as he cut the front lawn? He usually allowed you to steer, making quite a unique pattern in the grass.

CHAPTER SIX
A POSSIBLE CAUSE

At twelve years of age we sought help from a highly recommended child psychiatrist. Josh was diagnosed with ADHD as many children are today and he began a regimen of prescribed medications, Ritalin then Adderall and finally Concerta all of which did not seem to work as he would not take them as directed. He also was not always honest with the doctor as to the issues troubling him. This is the time that the con-artist in him began to surface. He would tell me that his days were fine; he was doing well in school when in fact his grades were not up to par. He destroyed warning notices that came in the mail and when his actual grades arrived we would get angry at him for not being truthful and he was punished.

His prescriptions were changed periodically, depending on how his body was reacting to them (but how can the doctor know if he wasn't honest in taking them?)

Josh often complained about an inability to sleep properly as well as some depression which continued throughout high school. He was never truthful about his emotions, never telling me what was really bothering him no matter how hard I tried to figure out his mental state. Most boys typically when asked "*How was your day*? The answer is "*fine!*" Whereas, girls describe their day in detail from sunup to sun down.

As Jill Bialosky states in her book "HISTORY OF A SUICIDE": *"For years, researchers have tried to find a genetic link for suicide. They haven't found it, but they have found evidence of a specific genetic link to suicidal behavior. In a 2000 study published in the American Journal of Medical Genetics, researchers found a mutation in a gene that regulates the brain's level of serotonin, a neurotransmitter that carries messages between brain cells and is thought to be involved in the regulation of emotion. They estimated that the mutation more than doubles the risk of suicidal behavior in those who have it."*

11/16/09

Dear Josh,

I have not written in a while…You are constantly on my mind. I have been asked to give lectures at different schools in the area talking about the dangers of drugs. I believe this will be good therapy for me.

11/17/09

Josh,

Uncle Alan called me at school this afternoon to tell me that poppy collapsed in their condo.

Grandma and poppy were out for lunch; upon coming home he collapsed in the entrance hall. Alan and I raced to the shore, making it in record time. The paramedics were called in the meantime, revived him and rushed him to the hospital. We arrived at the emergency room to total chaos. I recall running past other patients that were there for various reasons, one fellow was accompanied by two police officers as he was being treated and under arrest for drunk driving. Poppy was in the rear of the room attended to by many doctors trying to figure out his exact condition and to the proper action needed. He was originally unconscious, however, arriving at the hospital he began to awaken. The doctors recommended a new treatment of cooling a patient to avoid brain damage. This process lasted three days and when he was "warmed" he had noticeable loss of brain function. We agonized over the decision to "pull the plug" as poppy would **never** have wanted to live if he was not 100%. He had a difficult time visiting his 104 year old mother in a nursing home. He always said "*I do not ever want to be kept alive by artificial means.*" "*Why doesn't someone help these poor people?*"

Thanksgiving 2009

Dear Josh

Our immediate family had dinner together at grandma and poppy's condo in Monmouth Beach. We took turns visiting my father at the Monmouth Medical Center in Long Branch NJ. The dinner was somber and filled with much nervous laughter and chit chat. I guess we all had pent up emotions like a teapot about to whistle!

We as a family agreed all had been done for him. It was torture visiting him as he was fifty to seventy-five percent brain damaged. All he kept saying in a garbled, slurred manner was "*What happened*?" His head and eyes rolled around uncontrollably, perhaps seeking his family. He could not even swallow ice chips that I placed in his mouth resulting in the need for a feeding tube. He seemed very frightened at this point. The day after Thanksgiving our merciful decision was made. He was taken off his heart medications and he passed away peacefully in a morphine induced sleep. I miss him so very much too; I have now lost the two most important men in my life!

We sat Shiva (mourning period) at our house for 2 nights and everyone from all our friends and cousins and the people from my school came to pay their respects. We also had a memorial at the Channel Club for him –it was a wonderful celebration of his life. Frank Sinatra was on all during the dinner, Laura and I said many words about his quiet strength!! I trust you can show him around and make sure he sees Grandpa Irving, Josie, Grace and John there too. The thought of you all being together helps me get through all of this (if I didn't believe in the hereafter I think I would just lose it).

Grandma May was a mess when he first passed away, she didn't want to see anyone. Luckily, there are many people in the building that can look out for her as well as friends in town. Miss you so much. Love, Mom

December 7th

For my birthday (in a previous undated card) - this is the printed message on the card followed by Josh's own words. *If I knew as a child what I know now, mom, I probably wouldn't have made things so hard for you. I would have understood that you were looking out for my best interest-even though it may not have seemed so at the time. I would have known how difficult it is to let go, stand back and let someone you love learn from their mistakes. I would have realized how fortunate I was to have a mother who was always there for me, even after an argument, even after I'd said things I shouldn't have. While it's too late for a lot of things, it's not too late for me to tell you that I appreciate how loving you are, how giving you've always been…and that even though I may not always be good at showing it I love you very much. Happy Birthday*

Then he wrote in his own words: "**Mom, I hope you will read this card with your heart as you always do and** *know that there's not much more I could say. If I were to write you a letter, it would be probably identical to these words, but I thought the card was more colorful and attractive! Sometimes in life, things happen that are painful for everyone involved. But you can't unscramble scrambled eggs! However, I want you to know that I love you and couldn't imagine not having you around. I hope one day I will have the opportunity to help you the way you've helped me over the years. Now go back and read the card again, cry for a couple of minutes and enjoy your birthday to the best of your ability." Love Josh*

CHAPTER SEVEN

BARGAINING

"The normal reaction to feelings of helplessness and vulnerability is often a need to regain control:"

If only we had sought medical attention sooner…

If only we got a second opinion from another doctor…

If only we had tried to be a better person toward them…

Secretly, we may make a deal with God or our higher power in an attempt to postpone the inevitable. This is a weaker line of defense to protect us from the painful reality." Julie Axelrod (Internet)

Not all of Josh's life was sad as we spent summer weekends at our house at the shore with the Italian side of the family. Twenty people for breakfast or dinner was not uncommon. Swimming, bike rides and football games on the front lawn with cousins and uncles were a usual occurrence. Winter vacations in the Catskills or Florida. Religious celebrations were conducted with his Jewish side of the family. Passover Seders and Rosh Hashanah dinners were the norm –always spent with his grandparents, cousins, uncles and aunts beside our immediate family and he always enjoyed these traditions. I never thought of Josh as being a religious young man, however, when asked during a Passover Seder- *"why aren't flowers sent to Jewish people when someone in their family passes away?* I was stunned that he knew the answer! He responded *"Because flowers die."* "That is *why stones are placed on the headstones of loved ones at Jewish cemeteries.”* I was impressed that he knew this fact.

I remember vividly on a family vacation in Jamaica; Josh and his sister (10 and 7 at the time) went to the gift shop in the hotel. They came back to the room with their arms loaded with snorkels and swim fins and candy and remarked *"this is great we didn't have to pay for any of this...we just had to sign for it!!!!"*

Josh grew into an extremely handsome young man-tall, dark hair, blue/green eyes; a square jaw revealing a strong smile. He was quite the charmer and ladies' man. There was a very soft emotional side to Josh, as a young adult he thought nothing of sitting on the floor to play with his two young cousins. There was also an angry side to his personality, generally going through a few roommates over the years while in Florida.

He had a childhood full of hope and happiness; he just couldn't find his way. When asked what he wanted to be when he grew up Josh had no answer. He would have been a fabulous writer as Josh would always write a wonderful passage in every birthday or Mother's day card I ever received. I wish my son could have been able to use his stubborn streak to avoid the pitfalls that the future drugs caused. It was at this point of his life that his personality really changed as he was never able to *"morph"* into a normal teenager. See article: "**Inside the Teenage Brain**" by Dr. Jay Giedd. (Internet)

Dr. Giedd is a neuroscientist at the National Institute of Mental Health. *"Recently, he spearheaded research showing for the first time that there is a wave of growth and change in the adolescent brain. He believes that what teens do during their adolescent years—whether it's playing sports or playing video games –can affect how their brains develop."* *"So if a teen is doing music or sports or academics, those are the cells and connections that will be hard-wired. If they're lying on the couch or playing video games of MTV, those are the cells and connections that are going to survive."*

Dr. Giedd goes on to state: *"The frontal lobe is often called the CEO, or executive of the brain. It's involved in things like planning and strategizing and organizing, initiating attention and stopping and starting and shifting attention. It's a part of the brain that most separates man from beast. That is the part of the brain that has changed most in our human evolution, and a part of the brain that allows us to conduct philosophy and to think about and to think about our place in the universe…It's not that teens are stupid or incapable of things. It's sort of unfair to expect them to have adult levels of organizational skills or decision making before their brain is finished being built."*

"It's also a particularly cruel irony of nature," he states *"that right at this time when the brain is most vulnerable is also the time when teens are most likely to experiment with drugs or alcohol."* Sometimes when he is working with teens, *"I actually show them these brain development curves, how they peak at puberty and then prune down and try to reason with them that if they are doing drugs or alcohol that evening, it may not just be affecting their brains for that night or even for that weekend, but for the next 80 years of their life."*

Dr. Giedd continues: *"About the time of puberty, people start specializing."* *"They start deciding"* *"This is what I'm good at, whether it be sports or academics or art or music."* *"All the life choices, even though they are still there, start getting whittled away, and we have to start sort of focusing in on what makes us unique and special."*

"For a long time, we used to think that the brain, because it's already 95% of adult size by age six, things were largely set in place early in life." *"We now realize this isn't true; that even throughout childhood and even the teen years, there's enormous capacity for change. We think that this capacity for change is very empowering for teens."* *"This is an area of neuroscience that's receiving a great deal of attention."*

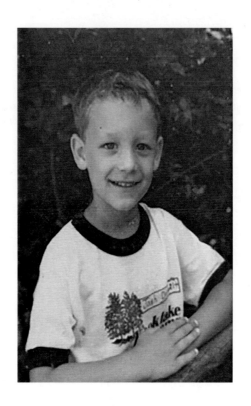

CHAPTER EIGHT
DEPRESSION
JOURNAL ENTRY

1/1/2010

Dear Josh,

   Sadness and regret are stages of depression that come when our loved one is gone. There are many, many times I wish I could hug Josh and tell him everything will be alright. That he did not have to end his life.

Not all people who are depressed commit suicide. There are specific medications to control depression, and as I stated earlier, Josh would not take them as prescribed or at all. These were huge erroneous decisions which led to a sense of hopelessness throughout his life.

I have been angry for the past few weeks- I don't know why or at whom (probably you). I still cannot believe that you committed such a horrific act-accident or not. Sunday will be the second anniversary of your death and it has been so hard for all of us. We feel as though we are in quick sand and cannot escape.

Dad and I have been going to bereavement meetings every month to try to make sense of this tragedy and it has been helpful for the time being.

We would walk into a small room in a local temple; sit on chairs that made a semi-circle in the dimly lit space. A candle would be lit by the facilitator and everyone would begin to tell or add to their story. I stopped going after about six months as I did not find it helpful. Perhaps this sounds a bit selfish. Whether it was a brother or girlfriend who committed suicide, or a father who shot himself or son who hung himself at summer camp, the outcomes are always the same. We as families are left to pick up the pieces of our fractured lives. As much as we tried to comfort each other we all left with the same feelings of loss and depression. I believe there isn't much that can be said to these people that will help them. Time is the only cure as the pain *never* leaves, it just becomes more tolerable. Perhaps it is "safety in numbers" that means something to each of them and that they do not feel all alone in this world. We as people tend to sit in judgment of each other perhaps to make ourselves feel better at the moment. We need to find the one thing that will help motivate us to move on with our lives. For me it is writing this book as this is giving meaning and a purpose to my life and yours. I will not let you be forgotten.

- Love you, Mom

3/27/10

Dear Josh,

Happy Birthday- I lit a candle for you today and will light another on Monday for Passover. I know you want your egg with Grandpa Irving's. Josh, this does not get easier with time and I trust you and poppy have found each other and are having a cigar!

Dad and I are growing apart as we are so different since your death. I feel as though I am constantly trying to hold him up from emotional drowning. Particularly, the eight years we dealt with all of your issues. Since your death we are like two ships that pass in the night, our feelings have changed for each other. I am only concerned for Jordan as I do not think she can handle a breakup.

- I love you always, Mom

CHAPTER NINE

FRUSTRATION

Josh attended 6th grade in a small school district; when we had the opportunity to move to a new town at the beginning of 7th grade. The transition to this town and new regional school must have taken a toll on Josh as he began to hang-out with the wrong kids. Not knowing the families and these children was a definite hardship and he began to make bad choices. I dreaded the bus coming up our hill as he usually entered in a foul mood and went straight to his room. Talking to him was impossible as he usually became very defensive and angry. We had many meetings with his teachers, tried after school tutoring sessions and eventually the grades improved. That was short lived.

At this point he began to self-medicate… only taking his meds as needed instead of regularly and often mixed them with illegal drugs such as marijuana and other pills. He made it through high school and even joined the basketball team but still did not have many friends. At the age of seventeen he began working at a local day camp where the campers adored him as he would take some of the troubled ones under his wing and try to understand their problems. Even though we **BEGGED** him to keep the job at the camp he chose to work at a local farm for higher pay. This choice was his downfall, even though he was living home with no financial responsibilities.

Money burned a hole in his pocket, as he needed a "fix" -buying something new whether it was sneakers, boots or jeans. I remember one incident where Josh went paintballing with some friends and **insisted** that I buy him a paintball gun and other assorted items. He would not take no for an answer at first. We would have a heated argument, however, after a few days of pouting that particular "obsession" would pass until the next one presented itself.

He stole money from my husband and I and often lied about his whereabouts-ex: one day I found a bat in his car, he said he was playing ball in the next town with some friends but he confessed later it was for protection when he was buying drugs in East Orange.

JOURNAL ENTRY

6/20/10

Dear Josh,

A few months ago I decided to stop wearing my wedding ring as I no longer feel married. Your sister often questioned why it is no longer on my finger and I answered – "too tight, it hurts at the gym etc." However, in reality I just don't want or need to be married any longer. Love You

11/11/10

Dear Josh,

Your father and I have been going through a very difficult time lately. Our marriage has suffered since your death. I am trying desperately to move forward in a positive direction. Dad and I had another very serious argument this evening and we are now in the process of a divorce.

Dec.26th 2010

Dear Josh,

I am feeling very agitated, angry and frustrated over my situation. I want my life back-not the old one but one where I can be independent and in my own place, have my own life and future. I need to feel a sense of contentment and security.

The fact that the holidays are here is not helping my state of mind. The only thoughts that help get through this nightmare is that Jordan is fine and handling our situation to the best of her ability. She is about to move out on her own and is very excited about the opportunity. I am also relieved that she does not have to make a decision as to whom to live with as I know she loves us equally.

This was also the first Christmas without poppy who among all the great things he accomplished in his life —he was a devoted Giants fan as are you and I. Remember the times when we would text each other and then call Poppy on every great play or not so great play. I miss our communications so much. Love You.

Dec 30th-Jan 2nd 2011

Dear Josh,

New Year's Eve was spent with Uncle Alan and Aunt Jude at grandma's condo. We enjoyed a great dinner followed by socializing with friends. I was surprised to realize that I had very few thoughts of dad with whom I had spent the last 28 New Year's Eve. I have had no regrets as to our recent separation and impending divorce. I feel as though I should have accomplished this departure sooner, but of course, hindsight is 20/20. I guess I just was not ready. Jordan spent the weekend with college friends in New England and she and I will be having dinner together this evening.

Today January 3, 2011 is the third anniversary of your death. Luckily, I am at work and being kept busy by my students. The days leading up to this day have been very sad and hard to get through. Yesterday was one of the most difficult. I still find this journaling extremely beneficial in getting through the dark times-my writings allow me to feel somewhat closer to you. I lit candles for you today - Aunt Jude had candles that say 'LIVE" "LAUGH" "LOVE" the last one to burn out was the one that said "LOVE". I know I probably read too much into all these "signs" but that is what gets me through each day.

CHAPTER TEN

"THE ANNILIATION OF ALL THINGS WORTHWHILE IN LIFE"

Josh attended a local university for one year and was asked not to come back. He missed a lot of classes and came home every weekend. During this time he was arrested by a local police officer for possession of marijuana in a school zone but because he was 18 we did not find out about it until we received a letter in the mail regarding a court date. My husband would accompany him to these court appearances and was shocked to see Josh's cocky and obnoxious demeanor. His punishment was only a fine as it was a first offence.

He did manage to have a girlfriend from high school who also attended the same college. She was a more diligent student and that relationship ended after the first year.

Josh did try to change his addictive ways by attending a local community college. That experience was a nightmare. I remember going with him one day to assist in the registration process. He could not handle this as he showed signs of confusion, anger and extreme agitation as we tried to look up at a large screen that displayed the classes being offered. *" I cannot handle this, I want to leave*" he said over and over. Josh only lasted a few weeks and was granted a medical leave. It was at this same time that Josh, wanting to get clean, considered joining the army, but instead entered a local rehab hospital on several weekends. The third time he was there we realized he was not making progress. So I packed a few clothes for

Josh, picked up my sister-in-law Jude, then Josh and it was now off to Silver Hill Rehab facility in Conn. He would be here approximately one –two months.

Jude has always been a very calming influence for our family, whether dealing with my daughter's health problems or mine to now dealing constructively with Josh. I knew he would not lash out at her.

On the way there Josh was extremely agitated; his knee was bouncing up and down relentlessly, he was speaking quickly and I could tell he wasn't sure about this change.

I know I would not have been able to stay calm with him for the entire ride, but Jude in her unruffled and composed demeanor could handle him. Josh kept repeating "*I must go home first!*" "*I must go home.*" We did not. We did stop along the way to buy some food and I was afraid he would not return to the car. Upon our arrival, he was calmer, perhaps seeing the facility made a difference or he just gave in. The registration process took forever, I just remember wanting it to be over quickly, as I began to see signs that he was getting impatient by his constant pacing. It was very late in the evening when we completed the paperwork. We said our good-bye's. This ripped my heart out. I cried all the way home; questioning all actions and decisions. "*How and why is this happening to us*?" "*We are good parents,*" "*Is this a personality disorder or just defiance?*" "*What did we do wrong, where did we fail?*"

As his parents; we were allowed to visit every weekend and near the end of his stay he was allowed home overnight. I was driving on the return trip, with my daughter in the back and Josh in the front. Not seeing anything out of the ordinary in his personality; ("*there was nothing ordinary about his personality!*") Approximately one mile from the facility which was situated in a mountainous, winding area he asked to drive. I said "*Okay,*" not seeing any signs of anger. He drove like a maniac, taking turns rapidly and I thought he was trying to crash with all of us in the car; however, at the last minute he came to his senses and slowed down. This event was terrifying for me as well as my daughter. He frequently displayed this "Jekyll and Hyde" side to his character.

In a letter to his sister during his stay there he stated: "*for years I suffered from this disease, and in return you did as well…with addictive illness comes* **the _annihilation_ of all things worthwhile in life**. *It brings misunderstandings, fierce resentment, financial insecurity, disgusted friends and employers, warped lives of siblings and sad companions and parents.*"

In her book "HISTORY OF A SUICIDE" Jill Bialosky reports "*Those who weather the storm sometimes emerge as people of talent and creativity; the birth of creativity can come from the risk of intense* **_self-annihilation_**. *And the sensitive, at times self-destructive tentative person is perhaps someone who lives at the balance of these two conflicting forces.*" Even though Josh was 23 years old when he committed suicide he was very immature. He was always taller than most children his age reaching adult height of 6'4" quite young. After his Bar-mitzvah at thirteen he grew six inches! Consequently, teachers, friends, and relatives always expected more of him. He could not step up and meet this challenge.

He was discharged after completing the program. It

was recommended that he enter an out-patient program in our area but instead after doing much research we decided on a half-way house in Fla. My husband took Josh to the airport hoping he would not change his mind. He did not. They successfully arrived at Boca House in Florida. At this point Josh began his long journey to get clean.

He would be there for approximately five years. He worked the program, eventually re-entered school and was given a job off the premises. We provided him with a small allowance every month as well as paying his tuition and rent after he was able to graduate from the facility. He traveled home on occasion and seemed to be on the right path. We were very encouraged at this point in his life; we really felt he was improving. He graduated from a local community college, entered Florida Atlantic University as a junior and we had such high hopes of him succeeding. Through years of psychiatric therapy he was finally diagnosed as having a *borderline personality disorder* as well as being an addict. I also believe he may have been bi-polar.

Josh continued in a positive direction for a brief period of time but just could not sustain it. Every time we said *"he's over the hump"* he would *"shoot himself in the foot."* By that I mean he was not mentally capable of making correct decisions. My bereavement therapist said it best *"You can see a physical disability in someone but not a mental one."*

I remember seeing his name or number many times on my cell or home caller ID and developing a knot in my stomach and not wanting to answer his calls. It usually meant he needed money for something or he was in trouble. One morning at about 5:00 am we received a call from him. He was on a college trip with a professor and other students in Costa Rica. He said *"Something bad happened!"* We responded *"What did you do?"* We learned that he had been locked out of his room and had to break a window and door to get in. In reality his roommate was frightened of his temper and locked him out on purpose. He paid for the damages but was not allowed to stay on the trip and immediately sent back to school. We were extremely angry and frustrated by his immature behavior.

On several visits home on weekends or holidays, Josh always brought his computer. A local business in the Boca Raton area hired many boys from the facility. He often stated *"I have many orders to process- I have a very important job selling diamond blades."* He usually felt inferior and intimidated around successful people. His "grandiosity" usually showed as he made himself out to be important.

One season in Florida he worked parking cars at a very fine beach club. The weather was extremely hot and humid. One patron of short stature and his young, sexy date pulled up to the club and Josh proceeded to take their car. Upon his departure this patron, seeing that the seat had been moved back said in an arrogant tone *"Do you know how much I paid for this car?* Josh replied *"Probably more that you paid for her!"* He was fired on the spot.

Josh began using steroids, along with Xanax and Oxycodone which changed his brain chemistry. This confused mental state continued to decline and he entered a terrible state of depression which caused him to neglect school and lose his job. He took out loans to enable himself to spend money on his bosses and coworkers in his imagined "grandiose" gesture of wild spending.

Throughout his young adult years in rehab and school he dated a wonderful young lady who was a gifted student as well as a positive woman in his life. She withstood many of his temper tantrums and outbursts; however, finally seeing a downturn in their future she ended the relationship. We had a final conversation with him on New Years Eve of 2007. We begged him to come home and try to turn his life around but he refused. At that point he could not see past this hurdle as the drugs made it almost impossible to think rationally. The dramatist in him came out for the last time as he went into a final sleep on January 3rd 2008.

"In most cases, suicide is a solitary event and yet it has often far-reaching repercussions for many others. It is rather like throwing a stone into a pond; the ripples spread and spread. ALISON WERTHEIMER, A Special Star (Internet)

The weekend of January 4th, 5th and 6th 2008

Josh passed away the evening of Jan.3rd. I received an e-mail that I did not read until the next morning- (perhaps that is why I had my cell phone with me.) He began this letter on a positive note stating that he would turn his life around by getting back into school and make better choices. As the letter went on it became darker and darker as he faced reality and knew these words were just hyperbole. He ended the letter stating that *" he loved me but just couldn't bear the pain any longer."*

Josh died suddenly, consequently an autopsy needed to be performed before his body could be released and sent home to us. This was a weekend filled with many heart-wrenching emotions. My family and Jerry's were in attendance, each offering support and as much comfort as possible under the circumstances.

Jerry's brother (Steve) and his wife drove down from Boston to be with us and assist in the arrangements. Steve had contacts in Florida that eventually aided in the release of Josh's body which was flown home on Monday morning.

The funeral would be Tuesday followed by "Shiva" (mourning period) at our home. I remember our immediate family being picked up by limousine to go to the chapel then eventually the cemetery. This process was excruciating, as we pulled into the chapel I saw the coffin in the back of the hearse and just lost it. *" I must be in a bad movie!"* *"That cannot be my son."* It was surreal. We entered the chapel and had a chance to view his body before greeting the visitors. I walked slowly and stoically up to the casket my eyes red and swollen. I stared upon my son still so handsome yet finally at peace. I kissed his cheek and touched his face; he was stone cold and pale. The receiving line was long, filled with family, friends, business associates and school staff and parents as well as their children. Our nephew and niece spoke during the service recalling some of the playful as well as the painful times in Josh's life. The cemetery was at least an hour away in Queen's, New York. This is where my husband's family members are also buried. The ride there was torturous and long with very little conversation as shock took over. The weather was a balmy 60 degrees and sunny on that January Tuesday "Josh always hated the cold." We had to walk a short distance to the gravesite. I remember seeing grave diggers standing nearby –just another job and day for them, but heart-wrenching for us as a family. He was buried next to his Aunt Lora who had passed away a few years earlier. In Judaism the tradition is to cover the coffin completely with shovels of dirt, first by family members then friends. I can still hear the sound of the dirt and stones echoing powerfully at first and then subsiding in intensity as they hit my son's casket. The return trip was just as somber filled with many tears.

The "Shiva" is supposed to be a time of remembering the loved one as well as a time to heal. Many, many people attended offering condolences and well wishes, but little could be said to comfort us. Children are not supposed to die before their parent's; it isn't the natural order of events. This period of time was exhausting yet somewhat comforting as I now believe Josh is free of the demons that took hold of his life. He is at peace. I returned to work soon after as it is my therapy; the smiling faces of my students help me get through the difficult days. The only other choice I had was to stay in bed with my head buried under the covers! This, I believe, would only have made things worse as I would not be able to think of anyone or anything else.

Question: Do you want your parents to endure this pain?

JOURNAL ENTRY

January 4th,2011

Dear Josh,

   Dad was served with the divorce papers today and our attorneys will talk next week. I am so much happier now that we are estranged and going our separate ways.

January 8th,2011

Dear Josh,

   I have been feeling very agitated and depressed for the past few days and have not been able to put my finger on the cause. I began to cry this am and now realize it is because of the frustration and anger over our situation that the court has caused.

   I have always been a structured, independent woman, however, now I am overwhelmed with the lawyers, my husband and the delays of the court system.   This situation has also caused some tension between your sister and I as I do not want to "bash" her father. However, she needs to understand my frustrations and anger at these circumstances. She and I have always had a close relationship and I do not wish that to change but she has stated in the past that I do not always understand her needs. She should put herself in my shoes, perhaps then she can understand my frustrations.

                                          -   Love you, Mom

January 19, 2011

Dear Josh,

I had dinner with dad's cousin Joyce tonight and was very surprised and elated to hear from her. I was a little apprehensive at first; I thought I would never hear from anyone on dad's side again. Love you, Mom

January 20, 2011

Dear Josh,

I had another panic attack at the end of school today. It seems they come on when I am under a lot of stress especially when I am under a strict time constraint. The Para-medics were called but I sent them away as it had passed by the time they arrived and I was able to go on with my day.

- Love, Mom

January 22, 2011

Dear Josh,

I went out for dinner with Mike and Linda this evening (remember-Mike introduced dad and I). We had a lovely time, we talked about our situation and how hard the last few years have been for all of us. "They" say the three most difficult events in life are: death (especially a child), a move and a divorce, well it seems I hit the *Trifecta* as I am going through all three within a relatively short period of time. I have to move forward in my life, whereas I believe dad is stuck and cannot move in a positive direction. At least that is how I perceive his situation, although I have not had any contact with him for over two months.

- Love, Mom

January 28th -29th 2011

Dear Josh,

I spent the weekend at the shore attending a relatives retirement dinner. I had mixed emotions as couples danced happily together on the dance floor. This was the first time I was alone and in this uncomfortable position. Couples were dancing to the oldies the way dad and I used to. This was the only time I was uncomfortable; I do not want to be treated as a third wheel as is the case of many divorcees and/or widows.

At one point the conversation turned to your cousin Alex who will inherit some of poppy's new clothes. I immediately thought of you. Alex and you are built alike; tall, muscular and extremely handsome. Oh how I miss you Josh.

It has snowed every week for the past month and I am very tired of its depressing image. I want and need spring. The feeling of warm sunshine on my face and the renewal of blooming trees, bushes and flowers is just what I need right now. This means a new beginning for me.

I enjoy exercise; however, walking in the snow is not for me, although I do it because there isn't any other choice. My sister-in-law and I "throw" ourselves on the floor and try to make it through and exercise video, however, we end up laughing and not accomplishing much!

February 11 2011

Dear Josh,

I had dinner with dad's cousin again last evening after journaling and working on this book. I know I read into odd occurrences' too often, but the light above our table kept blinking off and on. I trust this was you encouraging me to move on with this writing process. This day is significant in that it is three months to the day that I left your father. Our "motion" court date is set and I am hopeful that this will come to an end soon.

March 1, 2011

Dear Josh,

I received an e-mail from dad's cousin Barbara today. I so enjoy hearing from his relatives as they are all wonderful people. Dad's family is quite large compared to mine, poppy was an only child and grandma only had one sister. Whereas (as you are aware), dad comes from a much larger family including many aunts, uncles and cousins whom I miss a great deal.

- Love you much, Mom

March 8, 2011

Dear Josh,

I have not written in quite a while. I have been very busy with the divorce action as well as writing your story. If I can help one young teen or adult out there I will be happy. The writers group I belong to seems to think your story will become something...I'm not so sure but I do hope so. As I have stated all along this process is extremely helpful for me. I feel somewhat closer to you when I am writing. It's as if you are here in front of me guiding the way. I am at peace. I miss you so much. I love you

- . Mom

March 12, 2011

Dear Josh,

Jordan came over for dinner last night. I cannot help

but feel some tension between us, however, I never want to put her "in the middle" while we are going through our divorce. There are topics that I cannot discuss with her at this time, perhaps when things are finalized we will be able to discuss them. I do need to keep an open line of communication with your sister - this is very important to me. She and I have always had a wonderful relationship and I do not want that to change.

March 15, 2011

Dear Josh,

I had a very difficult discussion with your sister on the phone last evening. I tried ever so hard not to dwell about my impending divorce from your father. She and I agree that there is a wall between us lately. I really tried to listen to her concerns; she was only able to verbalize the fact that we aren't as close as in the past. She insists that I be honest with her about all issues regarding your father especially our court appearance this Friday. I gave her as much information as I believe she can handle at this point. There are other issues that I know she will be better able to handle in the future. She also told me that she feels bad because she sees her friends whose parents are still together. However, I am sure some of them have divorced parents as well. I tried to reassure that by the time she gets married (not even dating anyone at the moment) we will walk her down the aisle together. Jordan cannot see the positive future that is ahead of her. Instead she only sees the present and tends to dwell on it. As I stated previously, we tried to protect her from your problems as she had her own life to lead. Perhaps this was the wrong approach. Again, hindsight is 20/20. Love you

March 17, 2011

Dear Josh,

It is about 4:00 pm and I am sitting outside on Uncle Alan's deck the weather is a balmy sixty degrees. I guess I got my wish as I stated earlier in my journaling that I need warm sunshine on my face and to see the revitalization of trees and flowers. This transformation in seasons has definitely made my spirits brighter. I am not somber and depressed but happy and content. Love you, Mom

March 18, 2011

So happy, happy, happy.

March 19th 2011

Dear Josh,

I believe I have become somewhat intolerant to other peoples minor problems. I mean I have little patience for "bull-shit" issues. I do not want to hear "your nail appointment was changed; your tennis game was canceled, your husband will be late for dinner, you hit traffic on the way to work or you have the sniffles or are allergic to the smell in the nail salon." While in my nail salon, I was talking to the owner's daughter who also recently had brain surgery. I could not believe that she feels the same way that I do in regard to our lack of tolerance. Most people do not realize how fortunate they really are. They take their lives and their families for granted.

March 25th-26th

Hi Josh,

I am at grandma's house and becoming sad with the expectation of Sunday-your birthday. I lit a memory candle for you today. The anticipation of these milestones is very difficult more so than the actual day of the event. I think about you all the time. This memoir is helping me cope with your death as writing it gives me comfort.

Cousin Carrie called me to see how I am doing and to say she and her family are thinking of us on this day. I often wonder where you would be today, what your life would be like good or bad. I guess we will never know!

Our divorce is moving along, it should be finished in a few months. I just want to be alone.

- Love you, Mom

March 28th 2011

Dear Josh,

Our home went on the market today. It is just the day after you're birthday-quite emotional for me. I know the house needs to be sold so that we may move on with our lives; however, there have been happy memories there as well as sad ones. We moved there when you were entering 7th grade and your sister 4th grade. I vividly recall trying to help you put together a basketball hoop for the driveway. You were getting so angry at not being able to manage this feat as quickly as you would have liked. The neighbor from next door came out to see if he could be of any assistance as our conversation became quite heated as frustration set in. We were able to complete the job by nightfall.

May 1st 2011

Dear Josh

I have not written in a while… Ironically I moved back into our home on your father's birthday. Our divorce in moving along, not quite fast enough for me. This path has been difficult to say the least as it has been one obstacle after the next.

Your sister is handling it to the best of her ability. Her friends, her job in the law office and dating here and there are keeping her very busy.

Our home has been on the market for about a month or so, a few people have looked however, no offers as yet.

I feel as though I have poured my heart and soul into this memoir and I hope it reaches many teens as well as their parents.

June 21, 2011

Josh

   I am staying with grandma May for a few days as she is not well. She is now on oxygen and a nebulizer for more intense breathing treatments.

   A very strange event happened this morning. I came back from a walk and upon entering grandma's den I found a picture of me had fallen off the bookcase. There was absolutely *no* reason for this to have happened. This occurred after reading this story and dreaming of you last evening. You have been on my mind all day. I found myself looking at many pictures of you that I carry all the time and still wonder what we could or should have done differently. I still am seeking answers and always will. I miss you so very much.

                              - Love you, Mom

CHAPTER ELEVEN
ACCEPTANCE

Death can be sudden or totally expected. Reaching this stage is very difficult and a gift. Some of us cannot get beyond anger or denial. As I stated earlier, my anger comes and goes. This acceptance phase can be calming, often mixed with happiness and depression. I sometimes feel guilty for feeling happy. A balance needs to be reached to survive.

Our lives will never be the same as we constantly second guess ourselves. What could we have done to prevent this tragedy? Should we have been stricter? Softer? Given tough love? All of these scenarios play out in our heads over and over again. People tell us we did everything possible; the best doctors and programs but nothing worked. My husband, my daughter and I struggled with his drug dependency for 8 years leading up to his death. It has taken a huge toll on all of us in one way or another. My husband and I often were on different pages when we needed to make decisions on Josh's behalf.

My mother has been devastated by Josh's death to the point where only at this present time can I discuss his name without her crying. My father, at the time, went into total denial. He was so hurt and disappointed by Josh's action that we could not discuss him in front of my dad.

It has been many years since his death; we still have to take one day at a time, one hour at a time. Some days are better than others-the holidays are tough, his birthday is brutal and the anniversary of his death is horrific. But we are trying to move forward for our daughter, ourselves and rest of our family no matter how difficult that process may be.

Our entire family has been angry, sad and hurt upon having to accept his death. My relationship with my daughter is close; however, when I speak about divorcing her father she becomes very emotional. I have stayed in this relationship for HER and only HER. I trust someday soon she will realize that we both love her and I know she loves us; we just cannot live as husband and wife any longer. Even when Josh was dealing with his issues, we tried to protect our daughter. We did not discuss all the things that were going wrong in his life as she had her own life to lead. She always displayed a straight personality; never any problems with drugs, teachers, grades, etc. the model child. Jordan was in college at the time of Josh's death (in fact on a swimming training trip in Florida) when she was informed.

My husband once stated to our marriage councilor: *"I will be fine even if we do not stay together."* I hope this is true. I have been controlled emotionally and threatened verbally for the past few years; ever since I was no longer non-confrontational. It's ironic that ever since I began going to bereavement councilors and therapists I now have a clear picture of what I want out of life. I find I can stand up to my husband and challenge him on different issues; I was not able to do this before. I also was given another chance by surviving brain surgery. He has blamed my "issues" on that surgery as well as challenging my mental capacity. I have never been clearer in my thought processes; I have just tabled my feelings because of not wanting to hurt my daughter. I believe I have "pulled" him up for years from not "drowning emotionally in quicksand." As hard as I try to pull him to the surface he has fought like "a fish thrashing on a line" and I can no longer hold onto that line. It is time to let go!

EPILOGUE

MOVING FORWARD

The most important message I can tell you as my readers is: you only get one body and brain! Please, please take excellent care of them as there are **_NO_** do-overs in life. Yes, you may experience a broken bone or a medical disease and hopefully they will heel in time. Do not do anything to harm yourself.

Jordan, now an accomplished attorney, and I now have a solid relationship. Jerry and I, being divorced for quite a few years, now socialize with Jordan and her fiancé. We are anxiously looking forward to their wedding in September.

This path has been a difficult one and I am using all of my experiences to write this book. I am 69 years old and am not sure what direction my life will take; however, I am looking forward to the next challenging chapter of my life.

Printed by BoD™in Norderstedt, Germany

9 781956 074376